Only in Oregon

1995-2021: 26 YEARS OF OREGON POLITICAL CARTOONS

by JESSE SPRINGER

Only in Oregon: 1995-2021: 26 Years of Oregon Political Cartoons

Copyright © 2021 by Jesse Springer

All rights reserved. This book or any portion thereof may not be reproduced or used in any manner whatsoever without the express written permission of the publisher except for the use of example cartoons in a book review.

Printed in the United States of America

First Edition, 2021

ISBN: 979-8-9852087-0-2

Springer Creative
1574 Lawrence Street
Eugene, OR 97401

www.springercreative.com

Foreword

Drawing cartoons in Oregon is hard. Very hard. Why?

Well, there are all these different types of trees to draw. God help you if you get the old growth timber moss wrong or put spots on a Spotted Owl. Don't mess up the adipose fin on that steelhead! That Marbled Murrelet doesn't have wings like that. You will hear from every forester, wildlife biologist, and ornithologist in the state if you screw it up.

In 2012, I decided to be one of the few people in the history of migration to move from Oregon to California. In fact, my dear friend from high school in Minnesota became the governor of Oregon, so it was probably a propitious time to leave. I miss drawing cartoons about my former home, but fortunately we have Jesse Springer to carry on.

Jesse and I have drawn cartoons in parallel for decades. He would watch me, I would watch him, and somehow we didn't overlap. He noted that he wanted me to look at some of his cartoons 25 years ago, and I declined, because I was afraid his ideas would influence me.

Jesse is a rather unusual cartoonist, as he can actually draw. He does those trees correctly, I can assure you, for he lives in Eugene, where they really pay attention to this sort of thing.

Being a cartoonist is something you have to love. Trust me. It's very difficult to do. Jesse and I still think it's, you know, kind of important to spend some time on the artwork.

Jesse brings a still-fresh eye to the World Of Oregon, even as he is, gulp, Not From Here (New Jersey, Massachusetts) and has a very fancy psychology degree from Swarthmore College, which is like Reed College but without the giant slugs.

Enjoy Jesse's stuff. He's the nicest guy, wonderfully talented, even if he's from…sigh…the East Coast.

Wait! So was Tom McCall. Never mind.

— Jack Ohman

Author's Note

When I began drawing editorial cartoons about local issues in 1995, I dreamed that I would eventually work my way up to drawing cartoons on national issues, distributed nationwide by a major syndicate. At the time, the potential for such an aspiration was limited only by talent and hustle. I would make a living as an editorial cartoonist!

Sadly, with the advent of the Internet and the concurrent withering of newspapers' budgets, employment opportunities in the field of editorial cartooning all but disappeared. According to the Herb Block Foundation, where there were once 2,000 editorial cartoonists grazing the fruited plains of American newspapers, now there are fewer than 40, and the number is shrinking. My athletic talents notwithstanding, I stood a better chance of playing in the NBA than getting a job as an editorial cartoonist. I soon settled into my niche: by focusing on Oregon topics, I could meet newspapers' growing demand for "local" content while at the same time sell enough cartoons around the state to make taking off one day a week from my graphic design day job pencil out (sort of).

I have been drawing these Oregon-themed cartoons since 1995, and the result you hold in your hands is a 26-year whimsical illustrated history of the politics and culture of Oregon. This "greatest hits" collection of cartoons brings into stark relief the issues, both good and bad, that transpired in Oregon during that span. These are the issues that indeed make Oregon a special place. From what makes us unique — the "kicker" law, the timber wars and the lack of a sales tax, to what we pioneered during those years — Death with Dignity, vote by mail and the legalization of both marijuana and same-sex marriage. From the things that Oregonians are proud of — the beauty of its natural landscape and the prowess of its collegiate sports teams, to the things we're not so proud of — non-existent campaign finance laws, the PERS dilemma and an historic disinvestment in education.

During the past 26 years, Oregon has definitely become a blue state, although with decidedly strong red streaks. At once weird and traditional, urban and rural, liberal and conservative— Oregon is a place where the people are passionate and we are not afraid to voice their opinions. I have enjoyed assembling this chronicle of the political and cultural history of our beautiful state— by turns comical and controversial, but never boring— I hope you enjoy it too.

— Jesse Springer
Eugene, Oregon
October 31, 2021

How to Read This Book

All humor is context-dependent. When the bartender asks the horse, "Why the long face?" we have to know what a horse looks like to find that funny. (We also have to be at least 98 years old to have heard the expression "long face"). Not only are editorial cartoons context-dependent, but the specific circumstances surrounding their creation can be as fleeting as the cable news cycle. Here today, forgotten tomorrow. "What if I wasn't closely following Oregon political events in February, 2002," you ask? Never fear.

To help you maximize the enjoyment of this book, I have invented something I call "Instant Context." Above each cartoon is a dramatized (yet true to fact) "newspaper headline" to help put you into the frame of mind of the events of the time and place to which the cartoon refers. Once you've read it, you've got all the information you need to look at the cartoon and let loose an embarrassing, snorting belly-laugh.

Here are a couple of Instant Context tips.

1. Some people find it helpful to read the Instant Context **before** looking at the cartoon, and others say just the opposite. See which method suits you best.

2. Some of the cartoons aren't accompanied by any Instant Context because either the context is somewhat universal, or the cartoon itself supplies you with all the context you need. It's okay, just dive contextlessly right in.

3. For best results, read the cartoons in the chronological order in which they are presented because some Instant Contexts also apply to subsequent cartoons.

Enjoy!

New Property Tax Increase Measures Unpopular

February 1995 - Oregon lawmakers continue to depend on revenues from state sanctioned video poker.

Warner Creek to Be Logged After Arson

September, 1995 - The Warner Creek area, originally off-limits to harvesting because of environmental concerns, will now be logged as salvage timber after an arsonist set fire to the area.

Nike Signs Deal with U of O

February, 1996 - The University receives a huge payment in exchange for the prominent display of the Nike logo in University Athletics.

Pope Condemns Alleged Murderer's Taped Confession

June, 1996 - Despite the fact the suspect may have been confessing to a triple homicide, the Pope is more concerned with the man's right to get it off his chest.

Grateful Dead Disband

July, 1996 - After the death of band leader Jerry Garcia, the Grateful Dead have decided to stop touring.

Over Twenty Measures on this Year's Ballot

October, 1996 - Voters say the overwhelming number of initiatives makes it hard to remember which is which.

Soggy Weather Socks Oregon Again

November, 1996 - Record rainfall causes massive flooding across the state.

Tax Limitation Ballot Measure 47 Passes

February, 1997 - Lowered property taxes also mean cuts to some essential services.

Property Tax Limitation Measure Puts the Squeeze on Schools

March, 1997 - Meanwhile, funding for corrections remains strong.

God on the Side of Tax Reform

March, 1997 - Anti-tax crusader Bill Sizemore says that he is motivated by the belief that God wants people to have lower taxes.

Pay to Play

June, 1997 - Oregon's National Forests are beginning to implement a pilot fee program for recreational users.

Casey Martin Rides Again

February, 1998 - A Eugene judge allows disabled golfer Casey Martin to ride in a cart in a PGA event.

Republican Gubernatorial Candidate Bill Sizemore Has Questionable Financial Past

May, 1998 - The anti-tax crusader, who exhorts government to do more with less, racked up $800,000 in unpaid loans for a failed toy company.

Horror in Thurston

June, 1998 - Kip Kinkel murdered his parents before engaging in a school shooting at Thurston High School in Springfield, Oregon that left two students dead and 25 others wounded.

(USE THIS SPACE TO DRAW YOUR OWN CONCLUSIONS.)

Keiko Bound for Iceland

September, 1998 - Keiko, the orca star of the movie "Free Willy" and long-time resident of the Oregon Coast Aquarium, will be flown to Iceland where he will be returned to the wild.

Voters Overwhelmed

November, 1998 - A total of thirteen complicated and sometimes controversial ballot measures are on the ballot this November.

Oregon's Election Soufflé, Made Easy

INGREDIENTS

- TWO PHONE-BOOK-SIZED VOTERS' PAMPHLETS
- ONE HEAPING DISQUALIFIED BALLOT MEASURE
- TWO CUPS SLEAZY AD CAMPAIGNS
- ONE SCANT PINCH VOTER REGISTRATION FRAUD
- ONE HEALTHY DOLLOP OUT-OF-STATE SPECIAL INTEREST MONEY
- 3 TBSP. BORING RACES (YOU MAY SUBSTITUTE WITH UNCONTESTED RACES)
- ONE DASH QUESTIONABLE SIGNATURE GATHERING

DIRECTIONS

Mix ingredients four weeks ahead of time to allow flavors to fester. Bring to lukewarm on election day, then allow to cool for 2-3 weeks while the results trickle in. Garnish with lawsuits and legal challenges.

Serves: no one.

SPRINGER © 1998

springer@pond.net

Local Stores Closing

December, 1998 - Book stores and natural grocers in particular are feeling the competition from national chain stores.

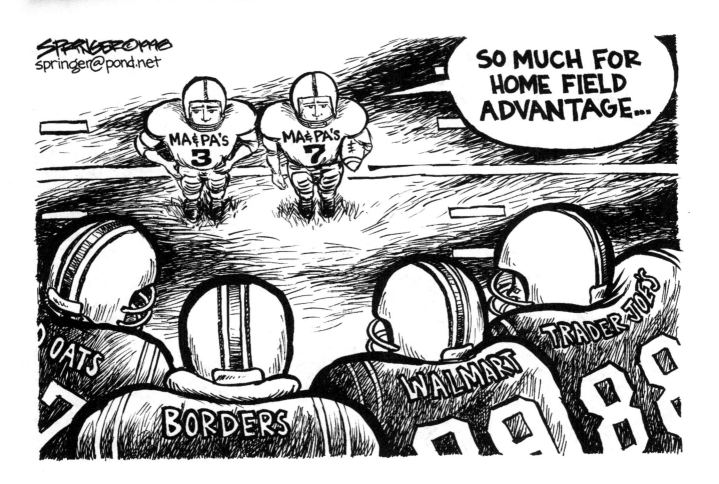

Freighter Runs Aground in Coos Bay

February, 1999 - The New Carissa freighter spills its fuel oil into sensitive wildlife areas on the Oregon Coast.

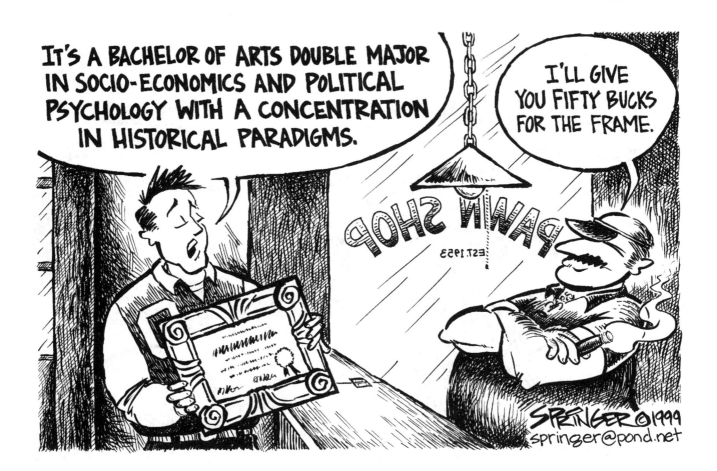

Kitzhaber and Legislature Constantly at Odds

April, 1999 - The GOP controlled state legislature opposes the Democrat governor's agenda at almost every turn.

WTO Protests in Seattle

December, 1999 - Many self-proclaimed anarchists from Eugene traveled to Seattle to participate in the protests against the World Trade Organization.

Y2K

January, 2000 - The new millennium begins!

Phil Knight Withdraws $30 Million Pledge to U of O

May, 2000 - The Nike owner is upset about the University's alignment with the Worker's Rights Consortium, a sweatshop monitoring group.

Dry Winter Leaves Reservoirs Low

May, 2001 - Water rationing in Oregon is likely this summer.

Attorney General Threatens Oregon's "Death with Dignity"

November, 2001 - Citing drug-trafficking laws, Attorney General John Ashcroft has promised to strip licenses from doctors who prescribe life-ending drugs, as allowed by Oregon's twice-approved Death with Dignity law.

Oregon Sends out $200 million in "Kicker" Tax Rebates

November, 2001 - Legislators approve the payout despite a forecasted $800 million budget deficit for the current biennium.

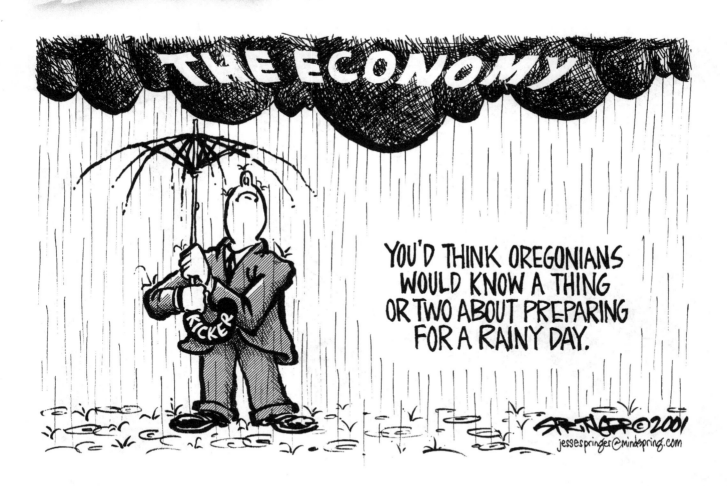

College Football Computer Rankings Pass on Ducks

December, 2001 - Despite the Ducks' #2 ranking in national polls, a computer formula has determined they won't be invited to the Bowl Championship Series' title game against #1 Miami.

Oregon Gains National Attention...
February, 2002 - ...both for its college basketball team and nation-topping 8% unemployment rate.

Class Sizes Grow with More Budget Cuts

March, 2002 - Property tax limitations are causing cuts the Oregon's public education budget, which is having a direct impact in the classroom.

Oregon Legislators Block Liquor & Tobacco Tax

March, 2002 - Despite strong popular support for "sin taxes" to help shore up the $800+ million budget deficit, the GOP-controlled legislature wouldn't even allow such a measure to be referred to the ballot.

Cigarette Tax on Ballot

September, 2002 - Oregonians will consider whether to raise the tax on cigarettes as a way to fund schools, police and other services.

More Gridlock in Oregon

September, 2002 - The bitterly divided Oregon Legislature has made absolutely no progress for ten days in a record fifth Special Session towards resolving the state's budget deficit.

Attorney General Still Gunning for Oregon Law

September, 2002 - U.S. Attorney General John Ashcroft appeals, to the 9th U.S. Circuit Court, a federal judge's decision to block the Justice Department from punishing Oregon doctors who assist terminally ill patients commit suicide.

GMO Labeling Measure Meets Stiff Opposition

October, 2002 - Biotech firms from across the country have mounted a massive spending campaign to defeat Oregon's Ballot Measure requiring labeling of all products containing genetically modified foods.

Oregon Voters Reject Measure 28

January, 2003 - The temporary, moderate income tax increase which would have prevented over $310 million in cuts to schools, public safety, and human services.

Oregon Budget Goes from Bad to Worse

February, 2003 - The state projects another $300 million budget shortfall for the last four months of the '01-'02 biennium, bringing the total deficit to $2.4 billion.

Oregon Lawmakers Reign in PERS Benefits

May, 2003 - Seeking to mitigate the crushing 25-year $16 billion shortfall of the Public Employees Retirement Program (PERS), legislators have voted to decrease retiree benefits, reneging on legally binding contracts.

Oregon's Problems Gains Notoriety

June, 2003 - Oregon's woeful economy and deplorable state of public education get attention in national news articles.

Look for these other exciting features!

▶ **From Clinical Trials to Free Drug Samples**
The Do's and Don'ts of Health Care without Insurance

▶ **Beware of Temping Trauma!**
6 Readers Tell Their Horror Stories

▶ **Getting Ready for a Fast Food Interview?**
Shed All Your Pride with Our 20-Minute Workout!

SUBSCRIBE TODAY!

Legislature at Standstill

August, 2003 - Partisan disagreements ensured the State Legislature would break the previous 208 day session length record, and Oregon is now the last state without an approved budget.

Oregon's Crowded Schools Get Worse

September, 2003 - Years of budget cutting have resulted in serious overcrowding in Oregon schools.

Domestic Spending Takes a Back Seat

October, 2003 - The U.S. Congress is currently considering a request from the Bush administration to approve $87 billion dollars for military and reconstruction operations in Iraq.

Puzzling Results

March, 2004 - Poorer Oregon counties, who stood the most to gain from a progressive income tax surcharge (Measure 30), rejected it by the largest margins.

Multnomah County Joins San Francisco

March, 2004 - Following the lead of San Francisco and other municipalities, Portland's Multnomah County has begun issues marriage licenses to same sex couples.

Anti-gay Activists Warn of a Slippery Slope

September, 2004 - Many supporters of an Oregon ballot measure that would define marriage as between one man and one woman claim that allowing gay marriage would be the first step in a slippery slope towards legitimizing all kinds of unorthodox marriages, including bestiality, pedophilia, and polygamy.

Video Gambling Bigger than Ever

December, 2004 - Oregon Governor Kulongoski announces a new state budget that relies even more heavily on state run video gambling to pay for police, schools, and critical services.

Bills Aim at Junk Food in Oregon's Schools

March, 2005 - Two bills introduced to the Oregon Legislature target the junk food sold in machines and concessions (and in the cafeteria) at public schools, in an effort to combat growing rates of obesity among school aged children.

Gay Marriage Foes Also Oppose Civil Unions

May, 2005 - After Measure 36 (gay marriage ban in Oregon, passed by 57% of voters) supporters explicitly allowed for civil unions during their campaign, they are preparing to fight newly introduced civil union legislation, saying now that civil unions are marriage in everything but name.

Oregon to Clamp Down on Cold Remedies

May, 2005 - With purchase limits of many common over-the-counter cold remedies already on the books, the Oregon Legislature is considering an outright ban on all OTC medications containing pseudo-ephedrine which is used as an ingredient in meth labs.

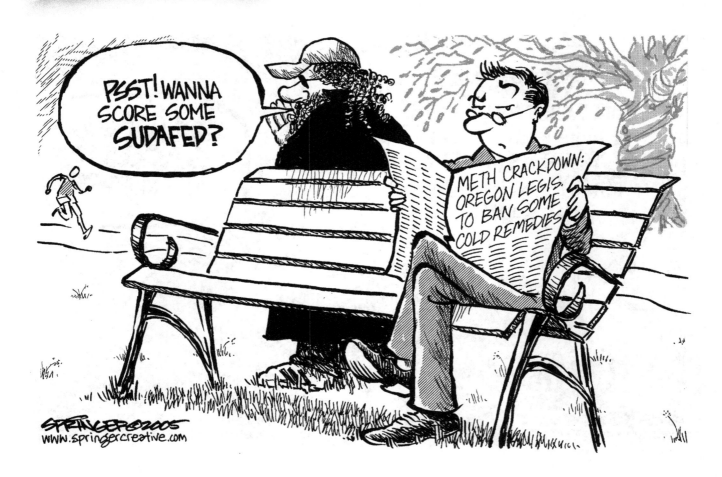

Scientists Weigh Protections for Native Plants

July, 2005 - Scientists are reviewing the endangered status of four plants native to the Willamette Valley.

SCOTUS to Decide on Oregon's Death with Dignity Law

October, 2005 - The Supreme Court begins hearing arguments in the Bush administration's challenge to Oregon's assisted suicide law.

Oregon Legislature Sits on Sidelines of Land Use Dispute

October, 2005 - Oregon's governor refused to call a special session of the legislature to solve the "land use issue" after a circuit judge tossed out a voter-approved property rights measure.

Oregon Judges Strike Down Ballot Measures

November, 2005 - Many Oregonians claim "judicial activism" is thwarting the voters' will, as several ballot measures passed by a majority of Oregonians have been struck down by Oregon judges.

Will Kitzhaber Return for a Third Term?

December, 2005 - Former two-term Oregon governor John Kitzhaber currently out-polls current Governor (and fellow Democrat) Ted Kulongoski on basis of his remark that he "would not rule out" a run for a third term in the 2006 race.

SCOTUS Upholds Oregon's Death with Dignity Law

January, 2006 - The US Supreme Court found that the Bush administration over-reached when it tried to apply the Federal Controlled Substances Act in an attempt to nullify Oregon's Death with Dignity Act.

Oregon's Kicker Comes Back

March, 2006 - During a time when schools, public safety and human services are suffering from drastic cuts, Oregon's kicker law (which goes into effect when revenues exceed projections by 2%) require that the state refund $665 million to individuals and corporations.

Lawsuit Demands Adequate Public Education in Oregon

March, 2006 - A group of families and school districts have filed a lawsuit against the state of Oregon and its legislators claiming they have failed their duty to adequately fund public schools, as is required by Article VIII of the Oregon Constitution.

Winners and Losers in Oregon's Water Wars

April, 2006 - Commercial salmon fishing off the coast of Oregon and Northern California will be severely restricted or maybe even eliminated altogether this year due to drastically diminished salmon runs from the Klamath River. The runs have decreased in large part due to irrigation water for Klamath Basin farms being drawn from the river in recent years.

Willamette Valley is Pollen Capital of the World

June, 2006 - The month of June is a time of suffering for about one third of the population of the Willamette Valley — the grass seed capital of the world.

OSAA Adopts "Competitive" Re-alignment

June, 2006 - Oregon Superintendent of Schools Susan Castillo upheld the Oregon School Activities Association re-alignment of high school sports divisions — to ensure competitiveness between schools — which will require many schools to travel several hours across the state, rather than across town to traditional rivals under the current system.

Oregon All in on Video Line Games

August, 2006 - With the addition of video "line games" to its state-run gambling offerings, Oregon grossed a record $1 billion dollars in gambling proceeds, putting it in the top ten of states in per capita gambling revenue.

Controversial Call Gives Ducks Victory Over Sooners

September, 2006 - The University of Oklahoma President has asked that the recent game between Oregon and Oklahoma, in which Oregon won by virtue of an apparent bad call by an official, be stricken from the record books. The replay official for that game has also received death threats from irate fans.

With Power Comes Responsibility

November, 2006 - One of the biggest challenges facing the new all-Democrat-controlled government of Oregon is enacting (and funding) meaningful ethics and campaign finance reform.

Oregon Rural Counties in Danger of Losing Federal Aid

February, 2007 - The Bush Administration claims that it cannot find the ongoing revenue to support funding for the aid to rural counties program.

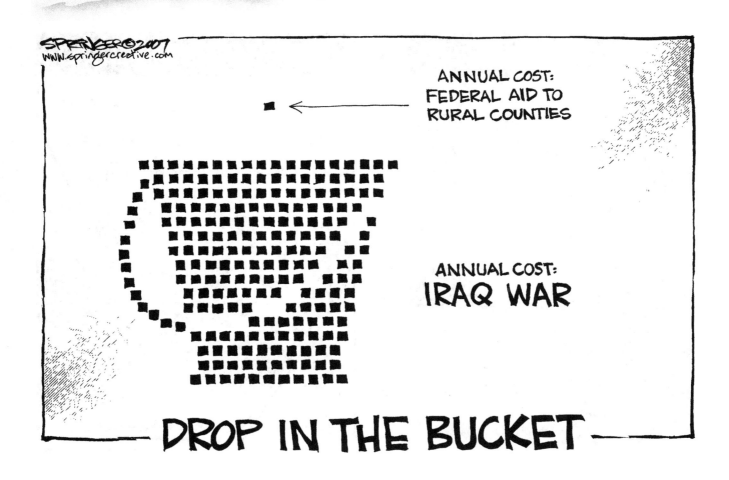

Oregon Cracks Down on Teen Phone Use While Driving

May, 2007 - An Oregon Senate panel passed a bill that would allow police to stop teenagers for using cell phones while driving.

Oregon Sees Gambling Windfall

June, 2007 - Oregon's budget has gone from deep deficits to surpluses, due in large part to a record $1.2 billion take from the Oregon Lottery, which includes video gambling.

Cheney's Involvement with Water Rights Runs Deep

June, 2007 - The *Washington Post* has revealed, in its eye-popping four-part series on the power and secrecy of Dick Cheney, that the Vice President (code named "Angler") was instrumental in pushing through a Dept. of the Interior decision (against the recommendation of the Fish & Wildlife Agency) to divert water from the Klamath River to area farmers. What followed was the largest fish kill the West had ever seen, with tens of thousands of endangered salmon rotting on the banks of the Klamath River, and 90% of the Oregon/California salmon fishery was closed-- the largest closure of its kind in American history.

Record Kicker Tops $1.1 Billion

September, 2007 - Oregonians will receive a record $1.1 billion tax refund because of Oregon's one-of-a-kind "Kicker" law which mandates the refund if revenues exceed projected revenues by 2% in any biennium. The law hinders the state from building reserves in boom times to provide for leaner years in the future.

Can Using Native American Mascots Be Respectful?

October, 2007 - An advisory panel has recommended to the Oregon Superintendent of Schools to mandate that Oregon public schools cease using Native Americans as school mascots, citing insensitivity to Native Americans in Oregon. A group of school administrators from around the state came to Salem this week to protest: they claim the imagery and use of mascots is tasteful and respectful.

Big Tobacco Breaks Oregon Campaign Spending Record

November, 2007 - Tobacco companies spent an Oregon record $12 million on TV advertising to successfully defeat Measure 50 which would have raised cigarette taxes 85 cents a pack as a funding mechanism to pay for health insurance for all children in Oregon.

Oregon Economy So Far So Good

November, 2007 - Despite a variety of gloomy economic indicators nationwide, Oregon is preparing to refund a record $1.1 billion "kicker" tax rebate.

Salmon Runs Lower than Ever

January, 2008 - The future of salmon fishing in Oregon is in serious question after officials report that salmon runs on the Sacramento River-- the backbone of salmon fisheries in California and Oregon-- are dangerously low.

Historic Legislative Session Uneventful

February, 2008 - The Oregon Legislature wrapped up its "test drive" of a legislative session a week early, without much rancorous partisan debate — or substantial progress on key issues.

Obama Coming to Oregon

March, 2008 - Presidential hopeful Senator Barack Obama plans a trip to Oregon.

Gas Prices Continue to Soar

May, 2008 - Setting new records almost every day, the national average for a gallon of gas is on the verge of $4 per gallon.

Federal Aid to Rural Oregon Dries Up

June, 2008 - A task force appointed by the governor has come to the belated conclusion that rural counties, and all Oregonians in general, are facing some dire straits without the renewal of Federal Aid to Rural Counties, which totaled $206 million for Oregon last year.

Bank Bailout Follows Crash

October, 2008 - The Bush Administration and Congressional Leaders are pressuring lawmakers to pass a $700 billion "financial industry rescue bill", otherwise known as a bailout.

Bill Sizemore Like the Energizer Bunny

November, 2008 - Despite sponsoring five ballot measures that all went down in defeat last week, perennial petition writer Bill Sizemore has already filed 13 new measures for Oregon's ballot in 2010.

Recession Officially Hits Oregon

November, 2008 - With a sudden jump in state unemployment to well above the national average, it is apparent that the national recession has hit Oregon.

Massive Stimulus Bill Flows to States

February, 2009 - Individual states try to figure out exactly how the $800 billion federal stimulus bill will benefit them as they sift through the 1,100 page document.

Lack of Savings Hurts Oregon

February, 2009 - As Oregon lawmakers scratch their heads and wonder how they will patch up the upcoming 2009-2011 budget with a projected $3 billion shortfall, they might regret the $1.1 billion "kicker" tax rebate they sent out in late 2007.

The Legislature Did What?

May, 2009 - The Oregon House voted 56-3 to make "Jory Soil" the Official Soil of the State of Oregon. With record unemployment and foreclosures rampant across the state, the people of Oregon heaved a collective sigh of relief.

Recession Trough for Oregon?

May, 2009 - Oregon's unemployment rate of 12% — second in the nation — remained steady, prompting speculation about whether we've seen the worst of the economic downturn.

Tax Measure May Go Before Voters

June, 2009 - The Democratically controlled Oregon Legislature is poised to pass an income tax increase to help balance its budget. Anti-tax groups have vowed to refer the tax increase to the voters, who have been historically reluctant to raise taxes on themselves.

Oregon Budget Does Not Reflect Harsh Economy

June, 2009 - The $15+ billion budget moving through the Oregon legislature relies heavily on Rainy Day Funds, one-time Federal Stimulus dollars, and a tax increase that is likely to be referred to voters and defeated.

Standing Trees Maximize Carbon Sequestration

July, 2009 - Studies show that carbon sequestration is dramatically reduced when trees are cut down, even in cases of thinning to suppress fire danger.

Timber Harvests at Record Low

July, 2009 - Timber harvests in Oregon for 2009 are approaching the record low of 3 billion board feet, set in 2001 (down from a high of 9 billion board feet per year in the mid 1980's).

Illegal Marijuana Grows Infest Rural Oregon

August, 2009 - Over 80 marijuana growing operations have been busted this summer in rural Oregon, mostly all of which have been connected with organized Mexican drug cartels.

Kitzhaber is Back

September, 2009 - Former two-term Oregon Governor John Kitzhaber throws his hat in the ring for the 2010 Oregon Governor's race.

Economic Recovery Can't Come Too Soon

September, 2009 - Oregon's unemployment matches a record 12.2%, even as signs of an economic recovery appear on the horizon.

Strange Days on the Oregon Coast

September, 2009 - Record temperatures on the Oregon Coast on the first day of fall were closely followed by the appearance of giant Humboldt squid, washed up on shore.

Swine Flu Hits Oregon

October, 2009 - Although health officials in Oregon aren't testing everyone with flu-like symptoms, they believe that the early season flu that seems to be striking so many people is probably the swine flu. While the seasonal flu vaccine, aimed at strains that appear later in the season, is available now, the swine flu vaccine will not be widely available for another few weeks.

Health Insurance Goes with Jobs

October, 2009 - An estimated 84,200 working age Oregonians lost their health insurance because of unemployment in the first 8 months of 2009. This is the highest rate of insurance loss due to unemployment in the nation.

Swine Flu Still Scary in October

October, 2009 - "Swine Flu" fears accompany trick-or-treating.

Hunger a Huge Problem in Oregon

November, 2009 - Oregon ranks second only to Mississippi in the rate of its population that went hungry in the past year.

"Class Envy" in the Eye of the Beholder

January, 2010 - Accusations of "Class Envy" have been made against supporters of Oregon's Measure 66 because it would raise taxes on only 3% of the most wealthy Oregonians. These accusations are usually followed by helpful suggestions that Oregon's budget shortfall could be (at least partially) solved if only state employees took cuts to their pay and benefits.

Legislature Steers Clear of Kicker Reform

February, 2010 - Although reform of Oregon's one-of-a-kind "Kicker" tax law would be the key to the state's future financial stability, the legislature was too timid to tackle the issue during a special session.

As the Stock Market Goes, So Goes PERS

March, 2010 - Oregon's Public Employees Retirement System (PERS) is only 80% funded, and without good performance from stock market investments, it will become an even bigger financial drain on public agencies around the state.

Oregon Tea Party Gets Ready to Demonstrate

April, 2010 - Anti-tax Tea Party demonstrations are planned across the state for April 15th.

Tea Party Demonstrations Widespread

April, 2010 - Tea Party demonstrations occur across America on "Tax Day", April 15th.

Oregon Has Lowest Childhood Obesity

May, 2010 - At a rate of 6%, well below the national average of 16%, Oregon ranks lowest in obesity rate amongst children.

Kitzhaber and Dudley Try to Occupy Middle Ground

May, 2010 - Primary Democrat and Republican front-runners in Oregon's governor's race are both trying to occupy the political middle ground as they look forward to November's general election.

Oregon Ready to Get Back to Boom and Bust

June, 2010 - After suffering through repeated boom and bust cycles, it looks like the "Great Recession" will keep Oregon in a "bust" mode without a subsequent boom for the foreseeable future.

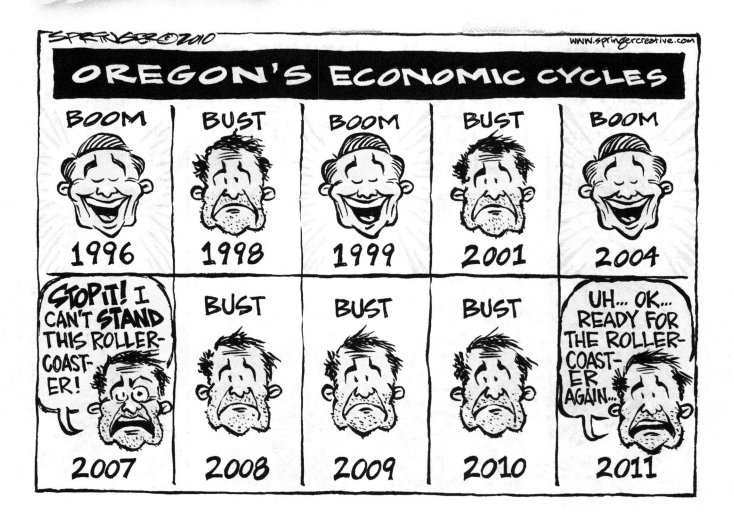

Oregon's Famously Short School Year to Get Even Shorter

June, 2010 - Already with one of the shortest calendars in the country, Oregon schools will once again be trimming days from the school year as a result of budget cuts.

Oregon's "Recovery" Not Recovered Yet

September, 2010 - Oregon's unemployment rate has been stuck at around 10.5% for 11 months. The good news? A year ago it was over 11%.

Oregon's Public Retirement Tiers Explained

September, 2010 - Due to contractually obligated but overly generous retirement benefits owed to Tier 1 (pre-2003) public retirees, the state of Oregon faces millions of dollars of liabilities which will necessitate cuts to schools, services and public safety for years to come.

Ducks Going to the "Natty"

December, 2010 - The Oregon Ducks go undefeated to earn their first ever berth in the National Championship Game, January 10, 2011 in Glendale, Arizona.

Ducks Lose to Auburn in Title Game

January, 2011 - The Oregon Ducks lose 22-19 to the Auburn Tigers in the BCS National Championship Game.

Oregon's Budget Deficit Looms

February, 2011 - Oregon Governor John Kitzhaber calls for "shared sacrifices" in his budget plan to overcome a $3.5 billion deficit for the upcoming biennium.

Obama Visits Oregon

February, 2011 - On a tour around the country to tout his initiatives for the second half of his first term, Barack Obama plans to stop at the Intel plant in Hillsboro to highlight a high-tech education program they sponsor.

Signs of "Improving" Economy Not Seen Across Oregon

May, 2011 - Although the signs point to an economic recovery for Oregon, the pace is absolutely glacial.

Oregon Educational System Crumbling

June, 2011 - In addition to projected layoffs of 3,000 school teachers next year, the state of Oregon is also raising tuition for the state university system by an average of 7.5%.

"Trickle Down" Economics All Dried Up

September, 2011 - While the grinding recession continues, middle class Americans wait for the "job creators" to do their thing.

Years of Cuts Take Toll on Oregon Schools

September, 2011 - Oregon will take advantage of President Obama's offer to allow states to apply for a waiver to "No Child Left Behind".

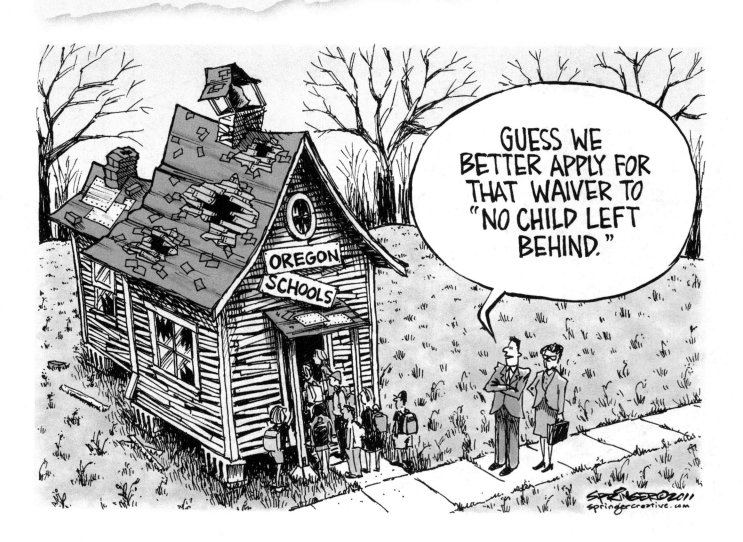

Occupy Wall Street Gains Traction in Oregon

October, 2011 - The "Occupy" movement sees swelling support, and events continue across Oregon.

Oregon Basking in Rose Bowl Glow

January, 2012 - The University of Oregon Ducks football team won the Rose Bowl for the first time since 1917.

Education Disinvestment Catching Up with Oregon Schools

January, 2012 - Oregon ranked 43rd in the nation in the latest "Quality Counts" project from Education Week, a respected annual report on the state of education in the United States.

Double-Whammy Hits Oregon's Rural Counties

February, 2012 - The economies of rural, timber-dependent counties are nearing crisis situations as they deal with a sharp reduction of timber harvests on federal lands coupled with an end to payments to rural counties from the federal government.

Some PERS Tier One Retirees Get Eye-Popping Payments

March, 2012 - Although the majority of PERS beneficiaries receive a retirement income that is proportional to their service in the state of Oregon, some retirees receive extraordinarily generous pensions as a result of some serious mismanagement of the pension funds in the 70's, 80's and 90's.

Sea Lion "Management" Halted for the Moment

March, 2012 - The states of Oregon and Washington had been set Tuesday to resume killing sea lions that eat salmon at the Bonneville Dam, but they instead agreed to hold off pending a legal challenge by the Humane Society of the United States. They contend that predation by sea lions has a small effect on salmon populations when compared with human influences such as fishing, hydroelectric dams and environmental degradation.

Native American Mascots Banned

May, 2012 - The Oregon State Board of Education voted to ban all Native American mascots at Oregon public schools. 15 schools around the state have until 2017 to remove the names and images of Native American mascots.

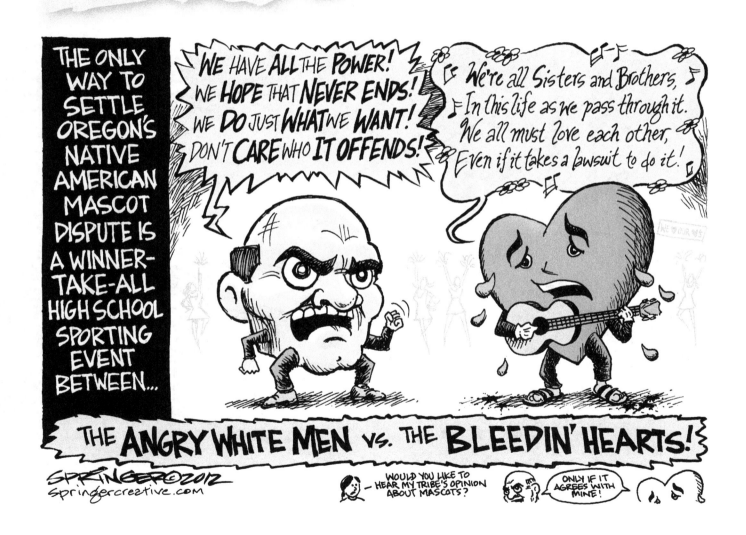

PERS a Persistent Problem

June, 2012 - Despite having a public retirement system that is more solvent than most states, payments from Oregon's public entities to Oregon's bloated PERS system comes at a severe cost to current public employees' ability to provide services to Oregonians.

Doobie-ous Ranking for University of Oregon

September, 2012 - Oregon ranks #4 in illegal drug use, a ranking that would surely rise if this fall's ballot measure to legalize marijuana passes.

Oregon All-in On Vote by Mail

October, 2012 - The first state in the Union to go all vote-by-mail sent out ballots to voters this week.

Oregon Tilts Democratic

November, 2012 - The Oregon House of Representative tips to Democratic control, making it a clean sweep for the Democrats: Governor, Senate, House, Sec. of State, Treasurer, etc.

Corrections Tops Education in Oregon Budget Pie

March, 2013 - At 10.9%, Oregon spends the highest percentage of its budget on corrections, and is only one of four states that spends more money on corrections than higher education.

Gun Control Gets Nowhere in Legislature

April, 2013 - Despite Democrats controlling both chambers of the legislature and a Democratic governor, it doesn't look like Oregon's legislature will even introduce a bill that seeks to limit assault weapons or high capacity magazines.

Gun Control Jams Up in Legislature

May, 2013 - Already watered down beyond recognition, it looks like the gun control bills will not get past this session of the Oregon Legislature.

Much Debated PERS Reforms Unlikely to Pass Legal Muster

May, 2013 - While Democrat and Republicans battle over just exactly how much to cut from PERS, Oregon's Public Employee Retirement system, a fierce legal challenge from retirees awaits.

Drought, Heat Increase Fire Danger

July, 2013 - Due to record scorching heat, fire season is officially declared in tinder-dry Oregon.

Cover Oregon Gets Expensive Hipster Ad Campaign

July, 2013 - Backed by a grant from the federal government, the state of Oregon paid $9.9 million for an ad campaign (currently featuring folksy guitar singers) to raise awareness about "Cover Oregon", the as-yet-not-operational health insurance exchange that will exist in Oregon in conjunction with the Affordable Care Act (Obamacare).

Age-old Timber vs. Environment Debate Rages Anew

August, 2013 - Timber companies and environmental groups are once again at odds as legislation to open up federal forest land to more logging is considered.

Curry County Refuses to Pay for Police

November, 2013 - For the second time this year, voters in Curry county defeated a tax measure to raise their property taxes (second lowest rate in the state) to maintain their bare bones level of public safety.

Cover Oregon Fails Miserably

November, 2013 - Once the poster child state for aligning with Obamacare, Oregon is now its biggest bust, admitting that the Cover Oregon insurance exchange will not be functional until after the December 15th deadline for individuals to enroll for insurance coverage effective January 1st, 2014.

Ron Wyden Proposes Timber Compromise

December, 2013 - Oregon Senator Ron Wyden unveils new timber harvest legislation that would supposedly strike a fair balance between environmental protections and revenue for timber-dependent communities.

Cover Oregon Still Not Operational Yet

December, 2013 - Despite millions of dollars and months of lead time, Oregon's health insurance exchange (Cover Oregon) has no estimate for when it will be operational.

2013 a Dry Year for Oregon

January, 2014 - Throughout much of Oregon, 2013 was the driest year on record.

Legislature Avoids Common Sense Gun Control

January, 2014 - Last year, universal background checks never made it to a floor vote in the Oregon Senate, despite polls suggesting broad public support.

Feds Look to Find Fault with Cover Oregon

March, 2014 - The Federal Government, responsible for the problematic roll-out of the "Healthcare.gov" site will conduct an investigation into what went wrong with the Cover Oregon health insurance exchange.

Is Cover Oregon Worth Saving?

April, 2014 - Oregon officials must decide whether to try and salvage the inoperable, bug-ridden healthcare exchange website provided by Oracle (at a cost of $200 million), or integrate with the federal exchange.

OR-7 Finds a Family at the End of His Long Trek

June, 2014 - After a 3-year, 1,200 mile journey, the Oregon wolf nicknamed OR-7 has found a mate and has fathered a litter of pups — the first known litter of wolves in southwestern Oregon since 1940.

Gun Control Opponents Get Nasty

June, 2014 - Oregon lawmaker Ginny Burdick received copious abuse — including a death threat — for proposing a law that would hold gun-owning adults responsible for crimes committed by a minor with their weapon(s).

Gun Deaths Outnumber Motor Vehicle Deaths in 2011

July, 2014 - Oregon was one of 14 states where gun deaths outpaced motor vehicle deaths in 2011, according to a study by the Violence Policy Center.

Kitzhaber's Nike Favor Pays Off

September, 2014 - Oregon's incumbent governor John Kitzhaber received a $250,000 campaign donation from Nike founder Phil Knight a year or so after he called a special session of the legislature to pass a bill giving Nike special tax exemptions that other Oregon businesses did not receive. Knight had donated $400,000 to Kitzhaber's Republican challenger in the previous election.

Kitzhaber's Re-election Bid on Shaky Ground

October, 2014 - A series of recent mis-steps means that Oregon Governor John Kitzhaber is going to have to rely on solid support from his democratic base if he is to be re-elected in November.

Spending on GMO Labeling Measure Breaks Record

October, 2014 - Money raised on both sides of the ballot measure to label GMO foods has broken an Oregon record, approaching $18 million. Over $11 million of that total was raised by the campaign opposed the measure, contributed mostly by biotech firms and large food producers.

Mariota a Lock to Win Heisman

December, 2014 - University of Oregon quarterback Marcus Mariota, always humble, soft-spoken and team-oriented, is the favorite to win the Heisman trophy.

Kitzhaber Stands by His First Lady Cylvia Hayes

January, 2015 - Oregon's First Lady Cylvia Hayes — already under scrutiny for possible corruption — now admits to accepting $118,000 form the Clean Economy Development Center while she was advising the governor on clean energy policy.

Kitzhaber Blind to Potential Conflict of Interest

February, 2015 - A series of revelations suggest a pattern of Oregon Governor John Kitzhaber's long-time girlfriend (aka First Lady) Cylvia Hayes using her position and influence for personal gain.

Kate Brown Sworn in as Oregon's Governor

February, 2015 - Replacing the resigning John Kitzhaber is Oregon's Secretary of State Kate Brown, who has been outspoken about her bi-sexuality.

Oregon Embraces Smarter Balanced Standard Tests

March, 2015 - Oregon schools begin implementing the new Smarter Balanced standardized testing, which is supposed to align with the Common Core curriculum.

Toxic Aerial Spraying Continues Unabated

April, 2015 - Despite numerous documented events of aerial herbicide sprays over forest land harming nearby people and animals, the Oregon Legislature refuses to take small steps to improve protections for neighboring groups.

Universal Background Checks Sparks Debate

April, 2015 - The Oregon Legislature is poised to pass a universal background check law.

COMMON GROUND IN OREGON'S GUN CONTROL DEBATE

Left speech bubble: SENSIBLE GUN CONTROL ONLY MEANS THAT CAN'T BUY A GUN IF YOU A FELON. IT WOULD BE NOT TO CLOSE THAT LOOPHOLE!

Overlap: YOU ARE WRONG

Right speech bubble: YOU CAN'T HAVE A FREE SOCIETY IF OVER-REGULATE GUNS & YOU PUTTING BURDENS ON THE PEOPLE. PRETTY SOON, ONLY CRIMINALS WILL HAVE GUNS!

Springer © 2015
springercreative.com

PERS Reforms Struck Down

April, 2015 - The Oregon Supreme Court rules that a majority of the reform to Oregon's PERS Public Retirement System passed by the legislature is unconstitutional because it violates a legal contract.

...IN ADDITION, THE **OREGON SUPREME COURT** RULED THAT EACH **PERS TIER ONE** RETIREE IS ENTITLED TO **ONE UNICORN** AS PROMISED UNDER CONTRACT.

HEY-- A CONTRACT'S A CONTRACT!

Oregon Ranks #1 in Athletic Department Revenue

May, 2015 - See how all of the University of Oregon's latest national rankings stack up.

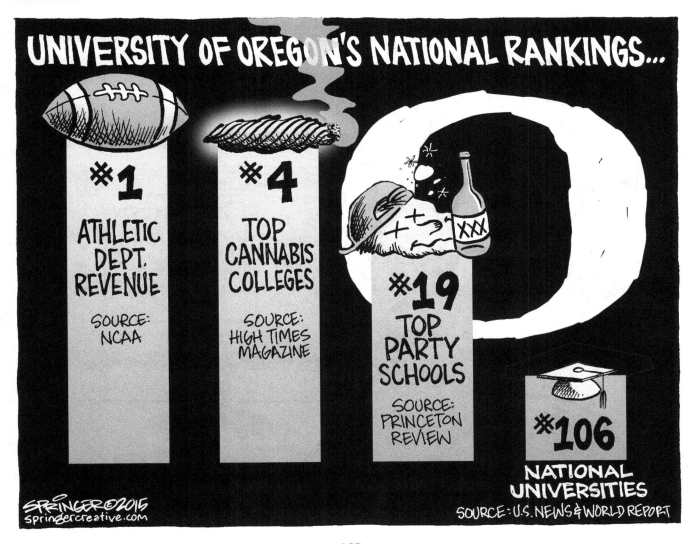

Heat Records Fall Again

June, 2015 - On top of a third year in a row of drought, Oregon experiences a massive heat wave with record breaking temperatures.

Pot Now Legal in Oregon

June, 2015 - On July 1st Oregon legalizes the use and possession of recreational marijuana.

Earthquake Article Rattles Readers

July, 2015 - The author of an article (in the *New Yorker*) about the Cascadia Subduction Zone says that everything west of I-5 would be "toast" if "The Big One" ever struck the Pacific Northwest.

Umpqua Shooting Revives Gun Control Debate

October, 2015 - The usual gun control debate follows the shooting at Umpqua Community College.

Sudden Change in the Season

December, 2015 - Oregon has gone from drought to drenched seemingly overnight.

Bundys Take Over Oregon Wildlife Refuge

January, 2016 - Cliven Bundy's sons Ammon and Ryan have led an armed occupation of the headquarters of Oregon's Malheur Wildlife Refuge as a protest against "federal tyranny".

Bundy Occupation Continues

January, 2016 - The occupation of Oregon's Malheur National Wildlife Refuge continues into its second week.

Bundy Occupation Drags On

January, 2016 - The occupation of Oregon's Malheur National Wildlife Refuge continues into its third week.

Last Hold-outs Surrender at Wildlife Refuge

February, 2016 - The last of the "patriots" occupying the Malheur National Wildlife Refuge are taken into custody.

Wolf Policy Falls Prey to Politics

March, 2016 - Offered as a political bargaining chip by Democrats to Republicans of the Oregon legislature, a law was passed to block the judicial review (that is required by Oregon statute) of the decision to remove gray wolves from the state's endangered species list. At last count, there were 11 breeding pairs among 110 known wolves in the state.

Trump Visits Oregon

May, 2016 - The presumptive Republican nominee for president Donald Trump pays a campaign visit to Oregon.

Hillary Bypasses Oregon

May, 2016 - The presumptive Democratic nominee is the only major candidate who hasn't bothered to pay a visit to Oregon during the primary campaign.

Primary Sees Low Turnout

May, 2016 - Despite record voter registration numbers, voter turnout for the May (Presidential) primary election was a very mediocre 45%.

Lawsuits Await BLM Timber Plan

August, 2016 - Both timber industry groups and environmental organizations are filing lawsuits against the BLM's latest timber management plan for Western Oregon.

High Volume Businesses Decry Proposed Tax Measure

September, 2016 - Oregon voters are set to decide whether to approve a massive "gross receipts" tax to pour badly needed money into schools and other services.

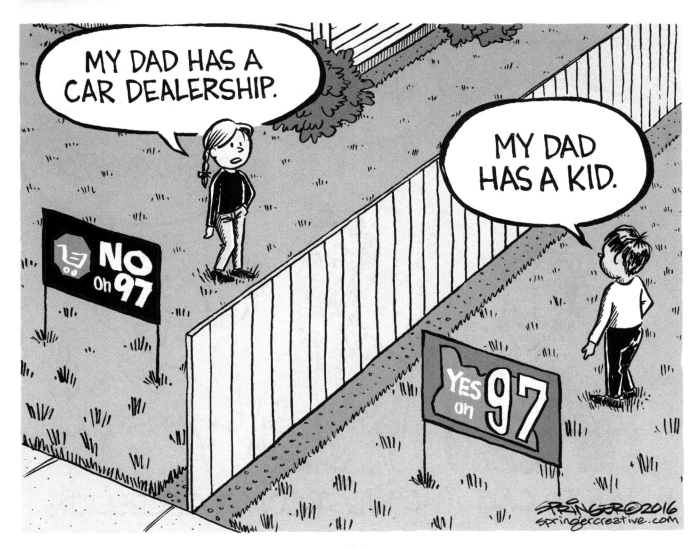

Donald Trump Elected President

November, 2016 - Despite a Trump victory, all the West Coast states voted for Hillary.

A House Divided

November, 2016 - Oregon's "Civil War" football game follows the divisive presidential election.

International Women's Marches Planned

January, 2017 - Protest marches across the country are planned for the day after Donald Trump's inauguration.

Oregon Doesn't Meet Emissions Goals

February, 2017 - Oregon doesn't come close to meeting carbon emissions goals.

Trump May Crack Down on Marijuana

March, 2017 - The Trump administration signals that it plans to enforce Federal marijuana laws in states where it has been legalized for recreational and medical use.

Trump Nominates Neil Gorsuch to the Supreme Court

March, 2017 - Donald Trump's nominee to the Supreme Court Neil Gorsuch has been outspoken against Oregon's Death with Dignity law.

Clean Fuels Debate Stalls Transportation Bill

June, 2017 - Disagreement between Oregon lawmakers about "clean fuels" emissions standards will likely derail badly needed transportation infrastructure legislation.

Roadkill Can Be Legally Harvested in Oregon

June, 2017 - Oregon makes it legal to harvest roadkill for food.

Kicker Saps Funds from Schools and Services

August, 2017 - Facing a multi-billion dollar budget deficit and schools in decline, the state "Kicker" law refunds $464 million in taxes, primarily to the wealthy.

More Smoke Settles in from Fires

September, 2017 - So far in Oregon, 24 wildfires have burned over 500,000 acres and choked the major population centers with thick smoke.

Sexual Harassment Claim Rocks Legislature

October, 2017 - Oregon state Senator Sara Gelser accused male colleague Jeff Kruse of repeated inappropriate touching and says there is a "culture" of sexual harassment in Salem.

Oregon Health Authority Bungling Again

November, 2017 - The Oregon Health Authority, which administers the state's Medicaid program (and was the entity in charge of the Cover Oregon debacle), has reported that it has recently made upwards of $150 million in over-payments.

Republicans Standing by Harasser Kruse

February, 2018 - Despite an independent investigation concluding that Oregon Legislator Jeff Kruse sexually harassed and groped multiple women in the state Capitol (after repeated warnings), he is not resigning and his fellow Republicans are not immediately calling for his resignation.

Marijuana Production in Oregon Sky High

February, 2018 - By some estimates, Oregon is producing three times more marijuana than is purchased in the legal market.

Oregon Counties Seek to Ignore Gun Laws

May, 2018 - Some Oregon counties are passing ordinances that empower their sheriffs to ignore any gun control law by deeming it unconstitutional. Three counties have passed them, and they may be on the ballot this November in seven more.

Stormy Daniels Makes National Strip-Club Tour

May, 2018 - As part of a national tour, performing at "gentlemen's clubs," Stormy Daniels makes three appearances in Oregon.

Trump Cracks Down on Asylum Seekers

June, 2018 - The 123 asylum-seekers who are detained in the Federal prison in Sheridan, Oregon are being treated worse than the non-immigrant inmates incarcerated there, and they have been denied access to lawyers.

Alt Right Groups Demonstrate in Portland

August, 2018 - Violent clashes between Alt Right "free speech" activists and counter protesters have become commonplace in Portland, Oregon.

Smoke Dominates Oregon Skies Again

August, 2018 - For the better part of August, unhealthy smoky air from forest fires has blanketed Oregon.

Oregon's Governor's Race Too Close to Call

September, 2018 - The governor's race in Oregon between incumbent Democrat Kate Brown and Republican challenger Knute Buehler is getting very tight, according to new polls.

Rain Finally Arrives

November, 2018 - At Thanksgiving, Oregon finally gets its first significant stretch of precipitation since the spring.

Massive Waste Found in Oregon Government

December, 2018 - An audit finds that the state of Oregon has been wasting upwards of a billion dollars per biennium by not using a modernized procurement system.

Creative Solution to Wolf Livestock Predation

February, 2019 - A cattle rancher in Southern Oregon is successfully warding off wolf attacks using two inflatable dancing men, given to him by the environmental group Defenders of Wildlife.

Should Oregon Lower its Voting Age to 16?

February, 2019 - The Oregon Legislature is considering a measure that would lower the legal voting age to 16.

New Bill Would Eliminate Single-Family Zoning in Cities

April, 2019 - In an effort to address Oregon's housing shortage, the Oregon Legislature is considering a bill that would effectively abolish single-family zoning in cities with populations above 25,000.

When it Rains it Pours

April, 2019 - After years of consistent drought, Oregon is getting well-above average levels of rain and snow, causing floods and landslides.

Legislature's Campaign Finance Bill Wouldn't Limit Much

May, 2019 - The Oregon legislature is crafting a campaign finance bill (Oregon is one of five states without any limits on campaign contributions) that would place limits on individual contributions but still allow unlimited contributions from political party committees.

GOP Walkout Denies Quorum, Stymies Climate Bill

June, 2019 - Republicans of the Oregon Senate have been out of the state for over a week in order to deprive the majority Democrats a quorum to vote on HB-2020, a cap-and-trade carbon reduction bill. There are roughly 100 other bills requiring a vote in the Senate before the session adjourns in three days.

Public Buildings Now OK in Tsunami Zone

July, 2019 - The Oregon legislature overturned a 25-year-old law that prohibits the building of new schools, hospitals, jails and police/fire stations in the Tsunami Inundation Zone. Scientists predict a 30% chance of a cataclysmic earthquake and tsunami in the next 50 years.

Climate Change Hurting Oregon's Fisheries

September, 2019 - A new United Nations report on the impacts of climate change gives a bleak outlook for the world's oceans. Oregon's coast has already been strongly affected, with acidification, low oxygen and warmer temperatures causing declines in shellfish, crab and fish populations — all important elements to Oregon's fishing industry.

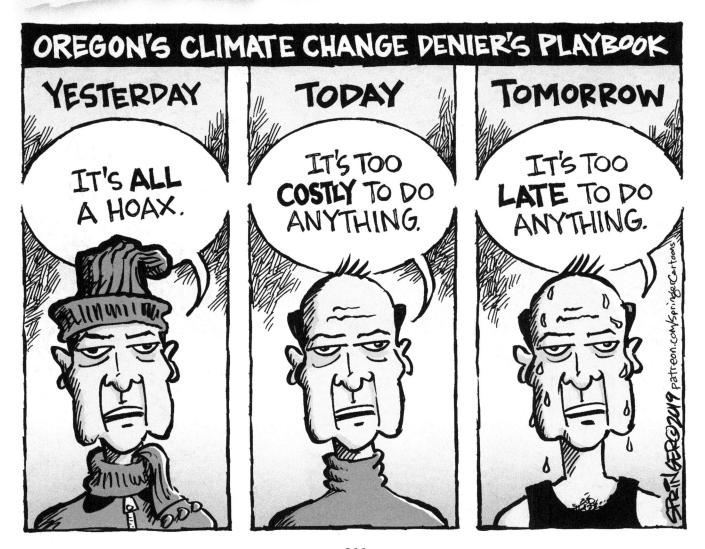

Vaping Linked to Many Illnesses and Deaths

October, 2019 - Following a national trend, eight Oregonians have had vaping-related illnesses, two of whom have died. Many in the health community are calling on the governor to issue a temporary ban on vaping products.

Oregon Women's Basketball Beats U.S. National Team

November, 2019 - The University of Oregon Women's basketball team defeated the U.S. Olympic team in an exhibition game. It was the first time a collegiate team beat the National team since 1999.

Oregon Bicyclists Can Yield at Stop Signs

December, 2019 - Oregon passes a law that allows bicyclists to treat stop signs as yield signs.

Ducks Win Rose Bowl

January, 2020 - The University of Oregon Ducks defeat the Wisconsin Badgers in the 2020 Rose Bowl by a score of 28-27.

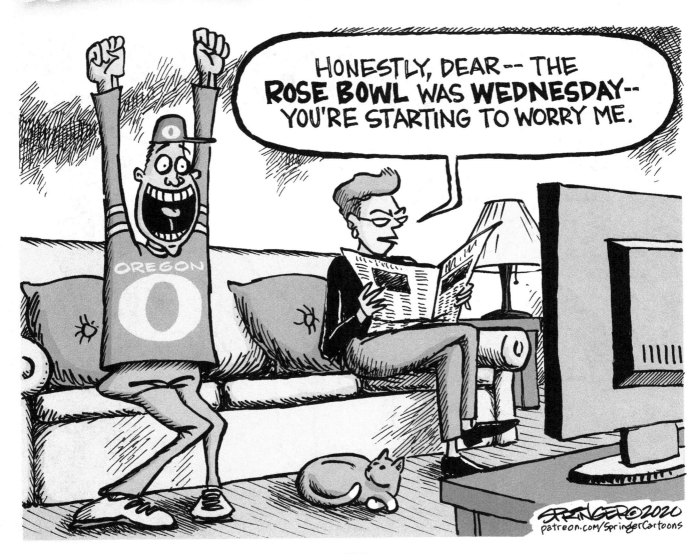

Oregon GOP Walks Out Again to Sink Cap and Trade Bill

February, 2020 - The Republicans of the Oregon legislature have fled the state Capitol to deprive the majority Democrats a quorum with which to pass a carbon cap and trade bill. They have their rural constituents convinced that if the bill passes, it will spell economic disaster for their communities.

Coronavirus Comes to Oregon

March, 2020 - Oregonians are bracing for the coronavirus as three confirmed cases have been documented so far.

CDC GUIDELINES ON SAFELY ENJOYING THE OREGON WOMEN'S BASKETBALL TEAM'S MARCH TO THE FINAL FOUR...

DO:
- Remain calm (despite historic season)
- Sanitize T.V. remote regularly
- Turn head 90° clockwise during chest bumps →

DON'T:
- High Five
- Hoard the snacks
- Share over-sized Foam Fingers

Toilet Paper in Short Supply

March, 2020 - Because of concern about the coronavirus, people have started to hoard toilet paper. As a result, toilet paper can't be found anywhere on store shelves.

Oregon Quarantine in Effect

March, 2020 - Like much of the rest of the U.S. and the world, Oregon ges into lockdown to prevent the spread of COVID-19.

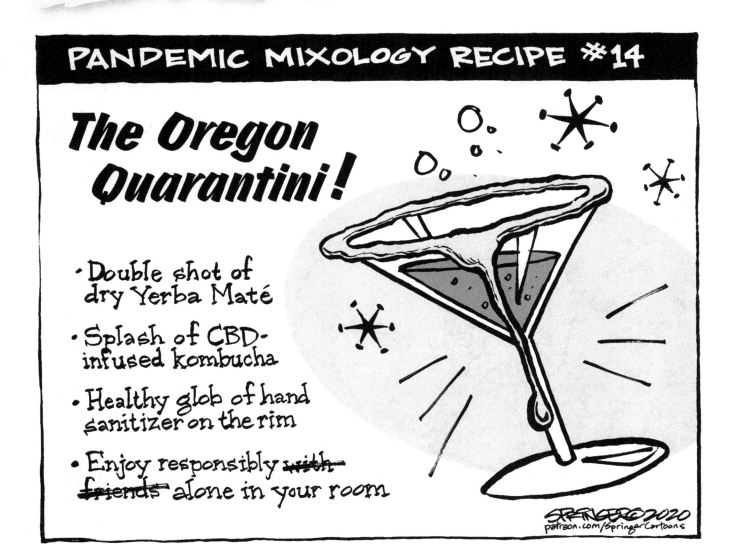

Most States Hunker Down Under Quarantine

April, 2020 - Like Oregonians, 90% of Americans are under a stay-at-home order in an effort to slow the spread of the COVID-19 coronavirus.

Oregon Quarantine Continues
April, 2020 - Oregonians adapt to life under quarantine.

Oregon Quarantine Into Fifth Week

April, 2020 - Many Oregonians are becoming resourceful as "non-essential" businesses remain closed.

Oregon Quarantine Nears Two Months
May, 2020 - Many families have been having lots of "together time".

Most Oregon Counties Begin Phase One of "Re-opening"

May, 2020 - Oregon has approved 28 of 36 counties for a "Phase 1" re-opening for businesses, which applies to restaurants, bars, gyms, salons and retail stores. Although social distancing measures still apply, gatherings of up to 25 people are also now allowed in those counties.

Despite CDC Recommendations, Mask Wearing Inconsistent

May, 2020 - As states continue to begin opening up their economies, a greater burden of preventing the spread of COVID-19 falls to personal choices and behaviors.

Almost All Oregon Counties Now Open

May, 2020 - As state restrictions ease, the responsibility for not getting or spreading the COVID-19 virus falls to individuals, as each foray outside the home now requires careful risk/benefit analysis.

Protests Spark Racial Reckoning

June, 2020 - The George Floyd murder causes more whites than ever to confront racism, both in society and in themselves.

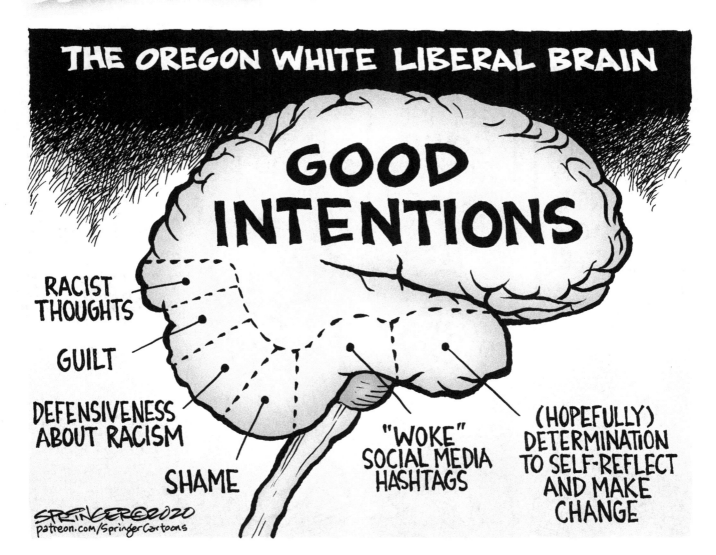

Virus-Preventing Behaviors Become Political

July, 2020 - Oregon's requirement to wear masks in indoor public spaces to prevent the spread of COVID-19 is seen by many as a political statement rather than a safety measure.

Federal Troops Descend on Portland

July, 2020 - After five weeks of consecutive protests in downtown Portland, President Trump ordered federal troops to disperse protesters. Portland police say they have no control over federal soldiers who follow orders from out of state commanders. While he was peacefully protesting, Donovan LaBella suffered a severe head injury from a "less lethal" munition fired by a federal agent.

Covid Fatigue Sets In

July, 2020 - A movement of awareness about racial inequity in America grows during the COVID-19 pandemic.

Oregon U.S. Attorney & U.S. Marshall Issue Joint Statement

October, 2020 - Individuals in Oregon law enforcement express a weariness about violence directed at them and would like it to stop.

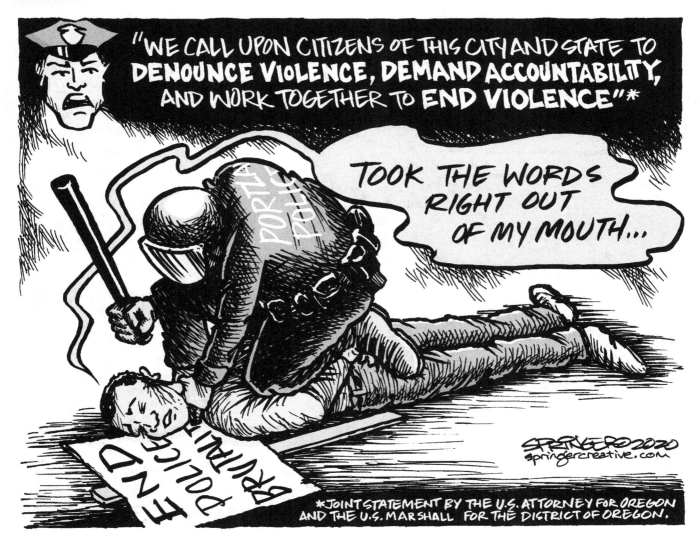

Psilocybin Treatment Legalized in Oregon

November, 2020 - Voters pass a ballot measure to legalize "Magic Mushrooms" (psilocybin) for therapeutic use in Oregon. A separate ballot measure passed that decriminalizes possession of small amounts of ALL recreational drugs, including psilocybin.

Fall COVID Surge Prompts Restrictions

November, 2020 - In the face of surging COVID cases and the approaching holiday season, Oregon Governor Kate Brown calls for a two-week "freeze", placing tighter restrictions on personal gatherings and some businesses.

COVID Restrictions Bring Backlash

November, 2020 - Many Oregonians criticize Governor Kate Brown's new restrictions as COVID cases surge and hospitals begin to get overwhelmed.

Death Toll Mounts in Oregon

December, 2020 - After breaking Oregon's monthly COVID death toll in November (300), the state is on pace to easily break it again in December.

Vaccine Arrives in Oregon

December, 2020 - The first doses of the COVID-19 vaccine are administered in Oregon.

Proud Boys Storm Salem, U.S. Capitols

January, 2021 - A couple of weeks after Proud Boys attempted to break into the Salem Capitol building to disrupt a session of the Oregon legislature, a Trump-inspired mob including many Proud Boys stormed the Capitol in Washington, D.C. while a joint session of Congress was counting the votes from the Electoral College.

Not Enough Vaccine to Go Around

February, 2021 - Oregon's phased-in roll-out of COVID vaccine eligibility is well ahead of the state's ability to distribute and administer the vaccine.

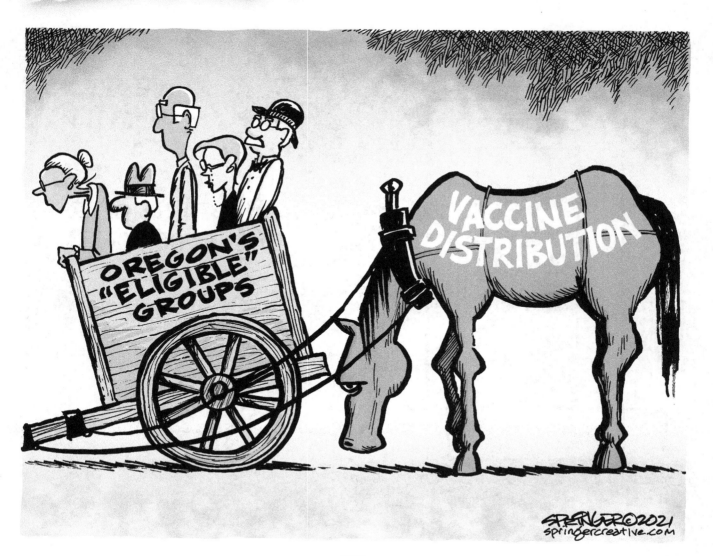

Vaccine Websites Vex Seniors

February, 2021 - In order to schedule their COVID vaccines, Oregon seniors have to navigate complicated online sign-up forms.

Oregon #1!

February, 2021 - Oregon ranks #1 in per capita internet searched for "armed groups" and conspiracy theories.

Vaccine Still in Short Supply

March, 2021 - Demand in Oregon for the COVID vaccine runs high among eligible AND non-eligible groups.

CDC Suddenly Changes Distancing Guidelines for Students

March, 2021 - Based on C.D.C. guidance, Oregon schools are now allowing a 3-foot distance between students in the classroom. While some families have already opted for remote learning for the remainder of the school year, many parents believe the new rules should allow a return to full in-person learning.

Oregon COVID Rates Going Up Again

April, 2021 - Just when it seemed like COVID was on the decline in the early spring of 2021, the delta variant, changing behavior and vaccination snags contribute to a "4th wave".

Oh, no-- you're at the end of the book!

Fortunately, there are two great ways to see even MORE cartoons!

1. Get every NEW cartoon sent to your inbox before they even get published!

For a mere $1/month, you can receive each weekly cartoon — hot off the drawing board — as well as the smug satisfaction of supporting the creation of political cartoons, something newspapers are struggling to do. If you value political cartoons in general, and my cartoons in particular, I urge you to support the time and energy I devote to this endeavor by signing up today. With your help, I can continue creating my weekly cartoons! It's super easy, just visit **patreon.com/SpringerCartoons** and sign up now!

SCAN TO SIGN UP FOR CARTOONS DELIVERED TO YOUR INBOX!

2. Get the Complete E-book with all 650 cartoons, most of which are in full color!

In order to create a cartoon collection that wasn't the size of a phone book (remember those?) I had to edit out roughly 400 cartoons that I drew in the last 26 years. Ulp — there are some seriously great cartoons I had to leave out of this book! Not only that, to make a book that didn't cost as much as a mid-sized car (remember those?), I had to convert all of my color cartoons into grayscale. Fortunately, dear reader, you can get the entire, colorful, unabridged cartoon collection in an e-book by going to **springerdesign.biz/books**.

SCAN TO ORDER THE UNABRIDGED E-BOOK!

CPSIA information can be obtained
at www.ICGtesting.com
Printed in the USA
JSHW011553091221
21048JS00002B/3

9 798985 208702